JUST A MINUTE MEDITATIONS

Trusting in God's Love

BY KATHRYN J. HERMES, FSP

Pauline
BOOKS & MEDIA
Boston

ISBN 10: 0-8198-3473-4
ISBN 13: 978-0-8198-3473-7

Library of Congress control number: 2024936356

Cover design by Tisa Muico

Published by Pauline Books & Media, 50 Saint Pauls Avenue, Boston, MA 02130-3491

Printed in the U.S.A.

www.pauline.org

Pauline Books & Media is the publishing house of the Daughters of St. Paul, an international congregation of women religious serving the Church with the communications media.

1 2 3 4 5 6 7 8 9 31 30 29 28 27 26 25

Contents

Introduction

The most important thing to know in life is this simple: "God is love" (1 Jn 4:16).

Tragically the human race was robbed of this knowledge and experience in the Garden of Eden. In some sense, all of us now carry the burden of not being quite confident that God, who is love, actually loves us.

In the Gospel Jesus, sent by the Father, announces that we are loved more than the wildflowers and sparrows that God cares for. He whispers this love in quiet conversations, displays this love in dramatic healings, reassures us of this love at the Last Supper, offers this love in laying down his life for us, and remains with us in his love in the Eucharist.

The Lord's love is fierce, true, and tender. He reaches out to us before we call for help. In every place in our lives where we see failure and disappointment, every part of ourselves we label as unlovable, he writes: "I love you, and will always love you. Nothing can change that."

For many years, I couldn't pry open my frightened heart to believe that God could love me. I guess I unconsciously felt God hadn't been there for me when I needed him. I hadn't seen that his mercy had upheld me and carried me on when I had sustained the wounds of circumstances beyond my control. I had believed it. But its truth had not yet touched me.

Friend, maybe you are in this place, where you believe but do not yet know. Or perhaps life's storms have buffeted your soul, and you no longer have the strength to lift your head in trust. Or maybe you feel you need to show yourself worthy of being loved by God, or to re-earn the honor of his attentive tenderness. Maybe you just want a place to finally lay down your burdens before him. I invite you to allow the experience that these Scriptures and meditations offer to touch that fragile place in your heart.

This short booklet of meditation and prayer is a companion on the journey from the insecure place of fear and doubt to the courage that comes from true security in God's love. As you pray your way through these pages, you will be invited to greater trust through *relaxing* the ways you take control of your life, *releasing* anxious thoughts, *remembering* how God has shown he has our good intentions at heart, *resting* in God who cradles all of his creation in his love, and *reflecting* on how to find the traces of this love in the midst of the challenges of daily life. You will find this little book a useful companion for deeper prayer when beginning or ending the day, or while spending time with Jesus in the Eucharist in adoration. It can be a resource when you're struggling and a pick-me-up at the moment you need help to believe in love.

Dear reader, wherever you are in this journey of life, when you pray with the word of God, you are united to the millions of people who have prayed and reflected on God's love and found their security in him for thousands of years. Most especially, in those quiet moments God is with you in a special way. In these pages you will begin a journey that can continue into the future as you entrust yourself to the word of God. Remember, you are never alone.

May your confidence to trust in God's love be restored and renewed.

1

You Care Even for Me

> "Why do you worry about clothing? Consider the lilies of the field, how they grow; they neither toil nor spin, yet I tell you, even Solomon in all his glory was not clothed like one of these. But if God so clothes the grass of the field, which is alive today and tomorrow is thrown into the oven, will he not much more clothe you—you of little faith?"
>
> MATTHEW 6:28–30

I remember walking down a country road one warm, sunny spring morning. As I rounded a corner, I was stunned by wildflowers growing in patches near the road. When my eyes fell on them, my heart startled me: "God loves the wildflowers!"

Jesus didn't say, "If God cares so wonderfully for elegant roses or exotic birds of paradise or sophisticated orchids." He said, "If God cares for the grass of the field"—the wildflowers—with such tender attentiveness . . . I knew then that God cares for me.

That experience was during a time when I felt like a wildflower, insignificant and not needed for much of anything. But God picked out the simple wildflower that grows in infinite variety across the world to get his point across. If you doubt that God sees you, if you feel that you're no one special, look how he cares for these simple flowers that grow here and there and everywhere. God cares much more for you.

When I feel as unremarkable as a flower that grows wild in the fields, your care for me, O Lord, gives me confidence.

2

I Have Stilled My Soul

. . . I have stilled my soul,
Like a weaned child to its mother,
    weaned is my soul.
Israel, hope in the LORD,
    now and forever.

PSALM 131:2–3 NABRE

We are given here an image of our true identity: we were made to be at rest, contented, safe; to belong, to be held, to be known, to be seen. A weaned child embraces his or her mother not to be fed, but simply to be in her presence and surrounded by her love. You and I were made to draw near to God like this, to be in relationship with God who wonderfully made us from our mother's womb.

Even as adults, we are as vulnerable as a weaned child, embraced by God at every instant. We were created not to make it through life on our own, but to be cradled and beloved in the everlasting arms of God.

To trust concretely looks like this psalmist's choice to calm and quiet the mind's churning agitation and to surrender all attempts to solve life's overwhelming problems on his own.

With great peace, take a deep breath, and close your eyes to fears, needs, what-ifs, and sorrows. Take your gaze off the past and the future and focus it wholly for a moment on the Lord, who holds you in peace and safety. Though chaos may reign all around, for a weaned child there is only this place where everything is okay.

Father, I thank you for helping me find peace.

3

You, O Lord, Are Right beside Me

I say to the LORD,
 you are my Lord,
 you are my only good.
I bless the LORD who counsels me;
 even at night my heart exhorts me.
I keep the LORD always before me;
 with him at my right hand, I shall never be shaken.

PSALM 16:2, 7–8 NABRE

We humans are subject to a thousand insecurities. Our trust in God's love is eroded by concerns about appearance, status, or popularity. Some of us fear inadequacy, failure, or even fear itself. Others try to compensate for inadequacy through strength, power, and prestige. But let's face it: in some way we all wonder if we are enough. The long night hours, when sleep eludes us, are witness to our secret worries and tears.

Psalm 16 reminds us where our confidence comes from. When uneasiness engulfs our heart, we need a strong guide. Our minds, tossed on the winds of worry, need the anchor of God's wisdom. When we lie awake at night, the Lord reminds us that he is always with us.

Jesus is asking you to entrust to him your worries about not being enough. He is deeper than the emotions you feel and stronger than the problems you face. This psalm gives you strong words to pray with. It is a prayer of faith made with a certainty that is unshakable. As you meditate on the psalmist's words, proclaim with deep trust, "With the Lord at my right hand, I shall never be shaken."

Quiet my mind and heart, that I may awaken to the gift of your presence.

4

I Rely, Lord, on You Alone

> Indeed, we felt that we had received the sentence of death so that we would rely not on ourselves but on God who raises the dead. He who rescued us from so deadly a peril will continue to rescue us; on him we have set our hope that he will rescue us again.
>
> 2 CORINTHIANS 1:9–10

I woke up in the hospital. I didn't exactly expect to die, but I sure didn't know why I was there. An outpatient surgery had led to a stroke, and thus began the rest of my life.

In the next few days, I learned I couldn't stand up, hold a fork, or feed myself. Though I quickly made significant strides in my recovery, the emotional balance that I had before the stroke now eluded me.

They say that in our curses are also our blessings. Now many years later, I realize the "curse" of the stroke led to the "blessing" of realizing I could do absolutely nothing without God's power in me. Repeatedly, he directed me to rely on him instead of myself, because only he has the power to raise the dead. He is the power of resurrection, of new life, of a new hope. Day after day, when we place our trust in Jesus, he continues to rescue us. Without him we can do nothing, but with him we can do everything.

By myself I can do nothing, but with you, Lord, I can do all things.

5

Lord, If You Will, You Can Heal Me

> A leper came to him begging him, and kneeling he said to him, "If you choose, you can make me clean." Moved with pity, Jesus stretched out his hand and touched him, and said to him, "I do choose. Be made clean!"
>
> MARK 1:40–41

Even if we tried, we would find little in our everyday experience to help us fully comprehend what it was like to be a leper in the ancient world. As he approached Jesus, this leper was frightening to behold, dirty and his clothes in rags. He was probably thinking, "I'm unclean, and I don't really believe. Will you care? I'm not sure you would want to do something for me, but *if* you do. . . ."

At times you, too, might approach Jesus in this way—with a half-in, half-out, I'm-not-sure-if-you-see-me-or-care-about-me act of faith. You may feel that your situation is too messy, too far gone, too shameful, and that no one, particularly Jesus, would want to know about it. Perhaps your sins, or the sins that others have committed against you, prevent you from feeling able to look into the face of Jesus with bold confidence. Maybe you assume that you are just not important enough to be noticed.

Go to Jesus! Go even if all you can make is half an act of trust. Jesus will reply to you, "I who made you, love you, and am here to save you. How could I not meet you even halfway with all my mercy?"

Lord, if you will, you can make me clean.

6

Do You Really Love Me?

"The Father himself loves you. . . . As you, Father, are in me and I am in you, may they also be in us."

JOHN 16:27; 17:21

With these few words from the long discourse at the Last Supper the night before he died, Jesus calms our greatest fear. I can imagine Jesus looking around at his closest followers that night, gazing at them with fondness, remembering their friendship over the past three years, appreciating how each has grown. I can't imagine how it must have been to be *seen* with this mysterious and loving gaze. We rarely experience total acceptance. Human love frequently gets rationed or withdrawn when we don't live up to another's expectations.

We may wonder: "Am I loved? Is there anything in me that God would love?" Yet even when we mess up, even if we totally blow it, Jesus still loves us and offers us his mercy. We forever belong to the God who is love. This is the "good news."

Jesus, I must confess I can hardly believe that this love exists for me. What is preventing me from receiving your gaze of love? How can I love you in return?

7

God Delights in Me

The cords of death encompassed me;
 the torrents of perdition assailed me.
He reached down from on high, he took me;
 he drew me out of mighty waters.
He delivered me from my strong enemy.
He brought me out into a broad place;
 he delivered me, because he delighted in me.
You have given me the shield of your salvation,
 and your right hand has supported me;
 your help has made me great.
You gave me a wide place for my steps under me,
 and my feet did not slip.

Psalm 18:4, 16–17, 19, 35–36

What would it be like to write the history of how God has reached down to rescue you? Do you remember times when God surprised you with something you had not asked for, something you eventually realized was exactly what you needed? It is by remembering the story, connecting the dots, cherishing the memories, and raising our hearts in gratitude, that we become ever more trusting that God is always with us.

In Psalm 18, the psalmist is doing just that. When we remember the times God has saved us, we can pray like the psalmist: "he delivered me, because he delighted in me."

If God *delights* in us, you can be confident that God is not abiding in the heavens while oblivious to you and your needs. No, his right hand will support you. His help will make you great. He will give you the shield of salvation. The Lord's eyes are on you; nothing escapes his notice. God is sovereign. God is faithful!

Lord of all, you delight in me.

8

For Everything There Is a Season

> For everything there is a season, and a time for every matter under heaven.
>
> ECCLESIASTES 3:1

One of the Bible's best-loved passages, this line from Ecclesiastes assures us that God has created an orderly world in which he has made everything suitable for its time. I have often written this verse in my journal when I am moving from one season of life into another.

Transitions mean letting go of what we have cherished and letting in new horizons. Sometimes we leave behind seasons of our life that have been painful; other times, we find ourselves walking into an era that we're dreading. God promises that when we are led down winding paths that make little sense to us, the situations we encounter are not random events.

When I am entering a new season, I take to prayer what God seems to be offering me in the coming years and how he might be challenging me to grow closer to him. I consider what values will be important to me and to others with whom I am living. Regularly reviewing these values has helped me to adjust my choices along the way.

When I intentionally involve God in how each season of my life unfolds, I discover that, even when I have feared a transition, God can be trusted. The way our lives work out is itself a mysterious expression of Divine Providence.

God of all promises, sometimes I don't understand where you are leading me, but I trust your promise to be with me always.

9

Lord, Do Not Forget Me

> But Zion said, "The LORD has forsaken me,
> my Lord has forgotten me."
> Can a woman forget her nursing child,
> or show no compassion for the child of her womb?
> Even these may forget,
> yet I will not forget you.
> See, I have inscribed you on the palms of my hands.
>
> ISAIAH 49:14–16

A newborn child soaking in a mother's smile doesn't need words to sense that love is the ground of all being. Yet we all know that the confidence a child has in his or her mother (or any parental figure) is often broken, sometimes through trauma or neglect, but most often because the parent has never personally experienced unconditional love.

Isaiah knows that inscribed in our very being is a thirst for a love that is infinite. We long for a love that is ours even if that most fundamental of relationships has been missing or ruptured, a love that can repair all the lack of love that has wounded our hearts through the years.

Take a moment to hear the Lord say the words of this Scripture passage to you by name. If you have lost the confidence that God loves you, if broken primary relationships have shattered your inner sense of being loveable, then this prayerful meditation, repeated often, may over time give you a new trust that God will be faithful to his word.

I praise you, Lord, for you have written my name on the palm of your hand.

10

Let It Be Done to Me According to Your Word

> The angel said to [Mary], "The Holy Spirit will come upon you, and the power of the Most High will overshadow you; therefore the child to be born will be holy; he will be called Son of God." Then Mary said, "Here am I, the servant of the Lord; let it be with me according to your word." Then the angel departed from her.
>
> LUKE 1:35, 38

Mary, a mere girl of perhaps fifteen, was told by the angel that she was to be the Mother of the Messiah. Then, after her *fiat*, the angel departed.

The radiant light that had surrounded the angel was gone.

She was alone in the room.

The assurance that she had been chosen by God to play a part in salvation history as the Mother of his Son was no longer right there before her eyes.

Mary's life was to be one of minute-by-minute trust. Trust in the promise when it was but a tiny infant who lay in her lap. Trust when a twelve-year-old announced he had to be about his Father's business. Trust when clouds of rejection circled around Jesus. Trust as he bowed his head and died. Trust as she laid him in the tomb. Mary, God's own Mother, had to walk with trust when she couldn't see, when all she had was a leap of faith.

Virgin of confidence, be my strength when I only have the courage to trust one moment at a time.

11

You Will Trample My Sins under Your Feet

Who is a God like you, who removes guilt
and pardons sin for the remnant of his inheritance;
Who does not persist in anger forever,
but instead delights in mercy,
And will again have compassion on us,
treading underfoot our iniquities?
You will cast into the depths of the sea all our sins.

MICAH 7:18–19 NABRE

"I can't forgive myself." Have you heard those words? Have you said them yourself?

We humans have a sharp memory when it comes to how we've failed. Meanwhile, our memories of our goodness, of our kindness, of the sacrifices we've willingly made for others—these are all like a passing breeze. Though the Lord doesn't stay angry forever, I've remained angry at myself for years. Sound familiar?

The Lord is not like us. He delights in showing a love that never fails. When a small child runs up to her parent with something she broke and says, "I'm sorry," and "I love you," in the same breath, the parent's anger quickly passes. This is only the tiniest glimpse into God's love for us.

It is essential to remember that we are cherished by God, who takes the list of sins we've given him and tosses it into the ocean, where the record of our transgressions and failures just disintegrates and is no more. Micah wants us to know that we can trust in the complete forgiveness God offers us. Our guilt will disappear.

Father, no words can express my gratitude for the mercy you lavish on me. May you be forever praised!

12
Jesus, Remember Me

> Then he said, "Jesus, remember me when you come into your kingdom." He replied, "Truly I tell you, today you will be with me in Paradise."
>
> Luke 23:42–43

Jesus doesn't hold grudges. Period. Sometimes we fabricate a God who holds something against us that we did in fifth grade. Who can't forget a sin we committed in our teen years. Who eternally ruminates on a detour from faith that we took for a few—or many—years of adulthood. And yet, the attitude of Jesus toward the Good Thief is the attitude he has toward each of us. Here. Now. He harbors no grudge about our failures, detours, or rejections.

Imagine Jesus' love as he looked toward this repentant man dying beside him and asking for heaven. In practically his final breath, this thief begged Jesus for what our Savior had come to freely give!

Did Jesus feel at that moment a mixture of delight, gratitude, and joy? I have experienced such a loving gaze from Jesus, and at that moment, I knew I had been seen, I knew I was known to the very depths of my being, and I knew that Jesus loved me.

Ask Jesus that you too may experience the gentleness of his attitude toward the Good Thief, who begged for the very thing the Lord had come to freely give us all.

Jesus, remember me, and welcome me into your Kingdom.

13

Who Will Separate Me from the Love of Christ?

> If God is for us, who is against us? Who will separate us from the love of Christ? Will hardship, or distress, or persecution, or famine, or nakedness, or peril, or sword?
>
> No, in all these things we are more than conquerors through him who loved us.
>
> ROMANS 8:31, 35, 37

Paul wrote this passage after undergoing hardship, distress, persecution, famine, nakedness, and perils. He is almost jubilant in his proclamation that nothing he has endured can separate him from Christ's love.

However, we ourselves may feel that we lack that same kind of trust in the face of troubles that threaten to upend our lives. We may worry that we have failed.

It is important to note that Paul wrote the letter to the Romans toward the end of his life. His confidence in exalting Christ's triumph over his every suffering had been crafted over many years of reflection, experience, and prayer.

Your own confident trust will grow gradually as you take small but courageous steps of faith. You can begin right now by speaking the words of this passage into the face of whatever hardship you are living.

Lord, I believe that nothing will ever have the power to separate me from you.

14
Give Me a Second Chance

> [Zacchaeus] was a chief tax collector and was rich. When Jesus came to the place, he looked up and said to him, "Zacchaeus, hurry and come down; for I must stay at your house today." So he hurried down and was happy to welcome him. Zacchaeus stood there and said to the Lord, "Look, half of my possessions, Lord, I will give to the poor; and if I have defrauded anyone of anything, I will pay back four times as much."
>
> LUKE 19:2, 5–6, 8

Tax collectors were notoriously greedy, deceitful, unjust, and hard-hearted. Focused on using this world's goods to build himself up, Zacchaeus was preoccupied with sustaining the lifestyle he had created with the personal fortune he had amassed.

To this man who was heading nowhere fast, Jesus offered himself as a gift. By doing so, he was asking a question: "Will you receive me, accept me, welcome me into your life, as messy as it is?" In that moment Zacchaeus experienced Jesus giving himself to him, and he responded generously by giving half of his possessions to the poor and restoring fourfold what he had stolen.

We can have confidence that we, too, will be offered a second chance like this again and again—opportunities to be set free to love more lavishly, to reverse self-serving habits, in order to focus on the deeper joys that come with caring for others and living in uprightness and truth.

Jesus, I am happy to welcome you and begin living for what will bring me lasting joy.

15

Though I Have Not Seen You, I Love You

> Although you have not seen him, you love him; and even though you do not see him now, you believe in him and rejoice with an indescribable and glorious joy.
>
> 1 PETER 1:8

A woman called me the night before a major operation. She was afraid, but when I suggested praying together, she responded, "Me and God don't get along." Gently I asked her to remember just one moment at any point in her life when she had felt God's presence. Without a moment's hesitation she recounted an experience thirty years prior when she had been in Switzerland, standing on the porch of a hotel room watching the sunset. She had been bathed in beauty and had felt so close to God. I heard her sigh. I felt a new peace in her. We re-entered that moment, and there we prayed.

I have never come across anyone who had lost their trust in God who couldn't remember at least one instant when they had been touched by the Lord's love.

When you most need Jesus, yet you can't see him, when you don't believe that he is there for you, ask the Holy Spirit to help you recall a moment when you did believe. There is a secret to this practice. Entering a felt sense of God's presence in our past makes it easier to find him once again.

I relax in your arms, O God. Here is where I was always meant to be.

16

Do You Not Care That We Are Perishing?

A great windstorm arose, and the waves beat into the boat, so that the boat was already being swamped. But he was in the stern, asleep on the cushion; and they woke him up and said to him, "Teacher, do you not care that we are perishing?" He woke up and rebuked the wind, and said to the sea, "Peace! Be still!" Then the wind ceased, and there was a dead calm.

MARK 4:37–39

Our lives can be tossed about by political storms, by economic pressures, and by epochal changes so strong that they threaten the world's peace and the climate upon which we all depend. Grief, desolation, loneliness, injustice—there is no limit to the situations and emotions that can capsize the tiny boat of our life.

This Gospel story depicts Jesus' power over any storm that could rage around us. As he stands to face the wind and waves that have so frightened the disciples,

Jesus shows them that the wildest fears die down when we run to him and call his name.

The Eucharist is evidence of the care Jesus provides through the journey of life. When you receive Jesus in Communion, he is not sleeping *next* to you while you bail out the water from your boat. He is truly *within* you, and he is awake! Tell Jesus of your need for him. Have confidence that he will draw you safely to himself and see you through the storm.

Jesus, please give me the peace you alone can give.

17

I Feel the Fascination of Your Gaze

> As Jesus was walking along, he saw a man called Matthew sitting at the tax booth; and he said to him, "Follow me." And he got up and followed him.
>
> MATTHEW 9:9

That day, Matthew sat at the tax booth, probably busy with his self-interested pursuits. He was sitting in a world he had built for himself as a collector of taxes for the Roman empire, taxes taken from his own neighbors, taxes that lined his pockets with wealth his friends and family could not enjoy. Matthew might have had no intention of changing his attitudes, his situation, or his dreams, if it hadn't been for the gaze of Jesus. That gaze would make this day different from any that had gone before.

Love is conveyed through the eyes. We can tell from the way someone looks at us whether we can trust that person. There was something about Jesus' gaze that gave

Matthew the confidence to step away from the world of his own creation and decisively choose whatever following Jesus would entail.

Jesus sees us wherever we are in our life. He passes by and calls us to follow him. Under the power of Jesus' gaze, something within us melts. We may feel dumbfounded, confused, and unsure, yet we are irresistibly drawn forward to trust even when there are no clear horizons or guarantees. So fascinating is this gaze that we cannot but give ourselves over to this joy that has seized us.

Jesus, how sweet is your gaze upon me.

18

My Cross, O Lord, Is Heavy

> Jesus began to show his disciples that he must go to Jerusalem and undergo great suffering at the hands of the elders and chief priests and scribes, and be killed, and on the third day be raised. And Peter took him aside and began to rebuke him, saying, "God forbid it, Lord! This must never happen to you."
>
> MATTHEW 16:21–22

Jesus is no stranger to the cross. He spoke of it during his life. He prepared his apostles for the moment when he would be crucified and taken from them. After his resurrection, even now, his hands, feet, and side bear the wounds of the nails. He even told his disciples they would need to take up their own crosses if they meant to follow him.

No life is spared from the cross. Even those who seem the happiest and most fulfilled at some point bear their cross. When our cross grows heavy and, like Jesus, we fall beneath its weight, we can lose our confidence.

What kept Jesus going on the way to Calvary? He remained committed to everything God was working out during the painful journey that would lead to the morning of the resurrection.

When our crosses seem to be tearing apart the fabric of our life, sometimes all we can do is, like Jesus, remain committed to what God is bringing about in us, even if we can't see what it is. And that is enough.

Jesus, I will not leave you alone on the way of the cross.

19

Help Me Not to Be Afraid

> As Pharaoh drew near, the Israelites looked back, and there were the Egyptians advancing on them. In great fear the Israelites cried out to the Lord. But Moses said to the people, "Do not be afraid, stand firm, and see the deliverance that the Lord will accomplish for you today; for the Egyptians whom you see today you shall never see again. The Lord will fight for you, and you have only to keep still."
>
> Exodus 14:10, 13–14

It isn't that difficult to imagine what must have been going through the Israelites' minds at the edge of the Red Sea: "Why did we trust this man with our lives?" "Why did we think that there could be anything better in store for us?" "Wasn't it better to just stay where we were?"

When we can't escape from moments like these, when our trust is weak and our anxiety has gone through the roof, we can turn to this passage from Exodus and breathe in the Lord's words: "Do not be afraid, stand firm. . . . The Lord will fight for you, and you have only to *keep still*."

We may object, "No, I have to figure out what to do! This situation needs a plan, a project, a strategy. Where will I get the money? God may call us to act, but he also prompts us to be inwardly still, to pray, and to turn the situation over to him. Only if we have the courage to rely on him will we witness God working in the midst of the situation.

Lord, help me always to be sure of your immense love for me.

20

Let Me Hear of Your Steadfast Love

Answer me quickly, O LORD;
  my spirit fails.
Do not hide your face from me,
  or I shall be like those who go down to the Pit.
Let me hear of your steadfast love in the morning,
  for in you I put my trust.

PSALM 143:7–8

They say our greatest fear as creatures is the fear of death. I wonder, though, if an even greater fear is the uncertainty of judgment, concern about our eternal salvation. We may worry that no matter how hard we have tried to be disciples of Jesus, in the end our lives might amount to nothing.

I told a friend in hospice that she had been a good mother. And she *had.* But she shook her head as if to say she had failed in the most important role of her life. As if she couldn't believe that any of the good she had done was real, would be remembered by the Lord, would last forever.

Jesus will one day show you the beauty of even the tiniest acts of kindness you have done in your life. Each one of them is so precious to him, even those you have forgotten. A daily habit of recalling your moments of tenderness, courage, or mercy will fill your heart with renewed trust in God's love.

Thank you, Lord. Thank you for remembering me. Thank you for treasuring every moment of my life.

21

Keep My Eyes Always on You

> After the death of Moses . . . the Lord spoke to Joshua son of Nun, Moses' assistant, saying, "My servant Moses is dead. Now proceed to cross the Jordan, you and all this people, into the land that I am giving to them. I hereby command you: Be strong and courageous; do not be frightened or dismayed, for the Lord your God is with you wherever you go."
>
> JOSHUA 1:1–2, 9

This was the second time the Israelites stood at the boundary of the Promised Land. Forty years earlier they had sent spies to reconnoiter the land promised to them as an inheritance. The spies reported that giants lived there. The Israelites were terrified. They had no desire to battle giants. They "did the math." They took their eyes off the Lord and decided against taking the land promised them.

So for forty years, the Israelites wandered in the wilderness. There they experienced God's power and compassion, his presence, and a care more tender than that of a mother. Although they lacked everything they needed and every possibility of taking care of themselves, God nevertheless caused them to flourish. Now, as they stood once more on the banks of the Jordan, they had a second chance. God strengthened them: "Be strong. Do not be frightened. I am here."

Can you name the "giants" in your life that have led you to lose your trust in the Lord and take your eyes off him? What did God reveal to you in that experience?

I will not be frightened or dismayed, for you are with me wherever I go.

22

I Want to Go Where You Call Me

> Now the Lord said to Abram, "Go from your country and your kindred and your father's house to the land that I will show you. I will make of you a great nation, and I will bless you, and make your name great, so that you will be a blessing. I will bless those who bless you, and the one who curses you I will curse; and in you all the families of the earth shall be blessed."
>
> So Abram went, as the Lord had told him.
>
> GENESIS 12:1–4

Precisely when Abram thought he was settled for the rest of his life, God offered him new horizons. On the surface, this might seem like a fine opportunity for Abram. He just had to go, and he would be given a country and prosperity. Great!

But . . .

Go where?

God called Abram to leave the security of everything he knew and travel to a "somewhere" he would be shown. Abram put his future into God's hands. He asked no proof, no guarantee why he should trust the God who was calling him forth. He just went.

Sometimes that is how it is. We simply must go. We just have to submit, to endure. When we walk into an unknown future with our trust placed in God, we, like Abram, will discover our true destiny, our authentic identity, and the reason we were put on this earth.

When you break into my life with something new, I want to go where you call me. In your hands, O Lord, is my destiny.

23
Father, I Have Sinned

> "'I shall get up and go to my father and I shall say to him, "Father, I have sinned against heaven and against you."' While he was still a long way off, his father caught sight of him, and was filled with compassion. He ran to his son, embraced him and kissed him."
>
> LUKE 15:18, 20 NABRE

There is an amazing detail in this parable: the father *ran.* When the father caught sight of his son returning home, he raced to reach him because his son's life literally depended on it. According to ancient custom, if a son lost his inheritance in a pagan land and dared to return, he would be met on the road to town by the villagers and declared cut off from his family and community. He would be considered as though dead. Therefore, this father needed to get to his son first. With this parable, Jesus reveals the heart of a lavish and merciful God who isn't waiting around until we return to him. He is reaching out to save us.

Whether the prodigal is ourself or someone else, this parable can give us confidence that God never rejects anyone. No prodigal is ever too far away to return. Even before we return to the Lord, we can be assured he is already running toward us!

Father, wrap all your prodigal children in your embrace and welcome us home.

24

Jesus, You Make All Things Work for Good

> We know that all things work for good for those who love God, who are called according to his purpose. For those he foreknew he also predestined to be conformed to the image of his Son, so that he might be the firstborn among many brothers.
>
> Romans 8:28–29 NABRE

Life unfolds amid peaks and valleys, the mountaintop experiences that fill our hearts and the unforeseen ordeals we can't even begin to understand. Like everyone else, I have often found myself reeling from difficulties and injustices that have caught me off guard. When these things happen, I take a deep breath, even as I shed some tears. Then I clutch these verses from Romans. It's not easy to whisper this *credo* when the heart is suffering. It often doesn't make me feel any better. It is, instead, a daring act of confidence that I repeat until God helps me see what he is doing.

As we look back at the valleys through which Jesus has shepherded us, we realize two things. First, God's purpose in calling us is very great: we are loved so much that, in all things, God is conforming us to his Son, drawing us into his inner life of communion for all eternity. Second, every piece of the puzzle fits. All things do work together for good. Everything belongs. Nothing is irrelevant. All is well.

Jesus, when I can't understand how something makes sense in the mystery of my life, I turn it all over to you.

25

You Laid Down Your Life for Me

"I am the good shepherd. The good shepherd lays down his life for the sheep."

JOHN 10:11

When Jesus speaks of himself as a shepherd, he affirms that he "lays down his life for the sheep." Notice, he does not say that he *will* lay down his life for his sheep, but that he *lays* it down. In the wilderness of life, the Good Shepherd protects and provides consistently, daily, today, now, for each of us and all of us together. When Jesus compares us to sheep who are such helpless creatures, he is trying to help us see how much we need him. Sheep are easy targets for predators like coyotes, wolves, and bobcats, as well as larger birds like eagles or vultures. A shepherd spends time with the flock to protect them against these predators. If a sheep rolls over onto its back, it cannot get itself upright again. Its four legs pointing up toward the sky, it begins to panic and within hours it could die. The shepherd carefully and gradually turns the sheep over and often rubs its legs to get the circulation going before allowing the sheep to return to the herd. Jesus is telling us that without the Shepherd's attentive eye at every moment, we would be lost.

Jesus, the Good Shepherd, loves us so much that he poured out his life, bringing us into the everlasting joy of God's life and love. In what ways have you experienced the Shepherd's attentive care?

Jesus my Shepherd, never abandon me. Keep me close to you, for I need you at every moment.

26

You Have Conquered the World

"I have said this to you, so that in me you may have peace. In the world you face persecution. But take courage; I have conquered the world!"

John 16:33

Jesus said these words to his disciples on the night before he died. Knowing all things, Jesus could tell his beloved friends not to be afraid, even though the distress of his death on Calvary was just the beginning of tribulations that would last until the end of time.

"Have great courage," Jesus told them, "not because someday I will overcome the violence and hatred in the world with my love. No! I *have* overcome the world!"

In the midst of the devastation of war, drug trafficking, slavery, violence in our streets, and brokenness in our homes, Jesus has established a new reality rooted in love.

Jesus' power is the power of a love that won't let us go, of a lover who lays down his life for the loved one. He is victorious over sin and hatred in the world because he has conquered the world with love. The kingdom of God is already at work, and one day all nations will bow before him.

When we believe this, we can cry out to those who divide and destroy, "We have confidence in the victory of Christ who loves us!" We can say to our soul, "Be steady and trust in the Lord." We can beseech the Lord, "Make me a channel of your peace in the world."

Jesus, nothing will stop the victory of your love in the world!

27

What Would You Have Me Do?

Saul, still breathing threats and murder against the disciples of the Lord, went to the high priest and asked him for letters to the synagogues at Damascus, so that if he found any who belonged to the Way, men or women, he might bring them bound to Jerusalem. Now as he was going along and approaching Damascus, suddenly a light from heaven flashed around him. He fell to the ground and heard a voice saying to him, "Saul, Saul, why do you persecute me?" He asked, "Who are you, Lord?" The reply came, "I am Jesus, whom you are persecuting. But get up and enter the city, and you will be told what you are to do."

Acts of the Apostles 9:1–6

Sometimes we truly mess it up. Saul thought that by persecuting the followers of Jesus he was honoring God. When Jesus appeared to him, however, it became abundantly clear that this was not the case!

We all have memories of things we've done or not done that even today make us cringe. It would be wonderful if we could make those things disappear! But despite our shame, this account of the calling of Paul the Apostle should give each of us great trust in God's love for us. When the Lord looked at Paul, he saw the person he had created him to be and the mission for which he was destined.

When you find yourself fixating on missteps and mistakes, turn your eyes to Jesus, for whom not one moment is lost and no detour is a disaster.

Jesus, what would you have me do?

28

I Welcome Your Gift of Love

> And during supper Jesus . . . got up from the table, took off his outer robe, and tied a towel around himself. Then he poured water into a basin and began to wash the disciples' feet.
>
> JOHN 13:2–3, 4–5

Imagine Jesus, surrounded by the apostles, standing up during the Passover meal, removing his garments and wrapping a servant's towel around his waist, pouring water into a bowl, and then kneeling before the others. How would you have felt if your Lord and Master poured water over your feet to wash them?

John's Gospel does not indicate the apostles' reactions except for Peter's: "You will never wash my feet."

Why was it important for Peter to let his feet be washed? Peter—and we ourselves— needed to learn that in following Jesus we don't proceed under our own power. In this gesture Jesus shows us that all we need to do is receive his gift of love, welcome it, delight in it, reverence it, surrender to it.

Jesus showed us in life and in death that the Father's love gives itself, bends over and serves, cleanses, and raises up. Our response is trust in him who lovingly pours himself out for us.

O Love that knows no beginning or end, I welcome you into my life.

29

Help Me to Live the Faith

> I solemnly urge you: proclaim the message; be persistent whether the time is favorable or unfavorable; convince, rebuke, and encourage, with the utmost patience in teaching. For the time is coming when people will not put up with sound doctrine.
>
> 2 Timothy 4:1–3

Confidence in God's love often looks like courage, the fearless conviction that the "message" we have received has meaning and that the world needs to hear it. What is this message that needs to be proclaimed? What does a world so confused and conflicted need to hear?

The message is this: God so loved the world that he gave us the gift of his own Son, that through Jesus' love in laying down his life for us we would be drawn to share forever in the joy of God's own innermost life.

Perhaps it is because people haven't encountered such a love in a real way that they pursue other "loves," mistaking as good what is actually destructive. I remember hearing a defendant in a trial state that his violent criminal activity was "who he was." "Oh no," I thought, "you are a child of God, who loves you unto death. That's who you truly are."

So be confident in this love of Christ for the world. As you have experienced God's love, go and share with others the love you have received.

How is it, O Lord, that you have loved me so much?

30

Your Mercies Begin Afresh Each Morning

"By the tender mercy of our God,
the dawn from on high will break upon us,
to give light to those who sit in darkness and in the shadow of death,
to guide our feet into the way of peace."

LUKE 1:78–79

Sunrise is a magical hour, when the sky trades its dark starry robes for the bright morning light. The pages of Scripture are peppered with references to morning, the rising of the sun, and the first light of dawn. They are symbols of God's faithfulness and glory—the hope that the security of God's love surrounds us even in the darkest of times. "The steadfast love of the Lord never ceases, his mercies . . . are new every morning" (Lam 3:22–23).

The verses from Luke spoken by Zechariah paint for us another type of dawn, the coming of Christ. He is the Dawn from on High, whose radiant rising dispels the power of darkness. The first light of every morning is only a faint reminder of Christ, the true Light of the World, who through his life, death, and resurrection has dispelled the painful shadows of sin and death. This dawn can be met with song: "Awake, O harp and lyre! I will awake the dawn" (Ps 108:2).

Never let a day dawn without renewing your trust in God's steadfast love for you.

Satisfy me in the morning, Lord, with your unfailing love, that I may sing for joy and gladness all my days (see Psalm 90:14).

Prayers

Psalm 16

Keep me safe, O God;
    in you I take refuge.
I say to the LORD,
    you are my Lord,
    you are my only good.
As for the holy ones who are in the land,
    they are noble,
    in whom is all my delight.
They multiply their sorrows
    who court other gods.
Blood libations to them I will not pour out,
    nor will I take their names upon my lips.
Lord, my allotted portion and my cup,
    you have made my destiny secure.
Pleasant places were measured out for me;
    fair to me indeed is my inheritance.
I bless the LORD who counsels me;
    even at night my heart exhorts me.
I keep the LORD always before me;
    with him at my right hand, I shall never be shaken.
Therefore my heart is glad, my soul rejoices;

my body also dwells secure,
For you will not abandon my soul to Sheol,
nor let your devout one see the pit.
You will show me the path to life,
abounding joy in your presence,
the delights at your right hand forever.

Psalm 16 NABRE

Prayer of Trust

O Heart of love, I place all my trust in you. Although I fear my own weakness, I hope all things from your goodness.

Saint Margaret Mary Alacoque

Prayer in Times of Anxiety

Father, I know that your love never fails and that you care for everything you have made. Whatever the troubles of our hearts, you guide and sustain us. May the beauty of your creation—the lilies of the field and the birds of the air (see Lk 12:24, 27)—be a constant reminder to me that nothing you have made is ever forgotten.

In moments of fear, give me courage; when I am overwhelmed by anxiety, give me renewed faith in your loving providence. I ask this through Jesus, your Son. Amen.

Jesus, Live in Me

Jesus Master—Way, Truth, and Life, *have mercy on me!*
Jesus, joy of my life, *live in me.*
Jesus, unconditional lover, *live in me.*
Jesus, life-giving bread, *live in me.*
Jesus, ever-flowing water, *live in me.*
Jesus, my all, *live in me.*
Jesus, my Redeemer, *live in me.*
Jesus, my deepest desire, *live in me..*
Jesus, who died for me, *live in me.*
Jesus, healing master, *live in me.*
Jesus, transformer of hearts, *live in me.*
Jesus, my beloved, *live in me.*
Jesus, gentle listener, *live in me.*
Jesus, faithful beyond death, *live in me.*
Jesus, suffering with your people, *live in me.*
Jesus, my delight, *live in me.*
Jesus, who calls me, *have mercy on me!*
Jesus, who molds me, *have mercy on me!*
Jesus, who challenges me, *have mercy on me!*
Jesus, who sends me, *have mercy on me!*
Jesus Master—Way, Truth, and Life, *have mercy on me!*

Marie Paul Curley, FSP

Act of Confidence in God

My God, I believe so firmly that you watch over all who hope in you, and that we will want for nothing when we rely on you in all things, that I resolve in the future to have no anxieties, and to cast all my cares upon you. "In peace I will sleep and I will rest; for you, O Lord, have confirmed me in hope" (see Pss 62, 63).

Others may deprive me of worldly goods and honors; sickness may take away my strength and the means for serving you; I may even lose your grace by sin; but my trust shall never leave me; I will preserve it to the last moment of my life, and the powers of hell shall seek in vain to take it from me. "In peace I will sleep and I will rest."

Let others seek happiness in their wealth and in their talents; let them trust to the purity of their lives, the austerity of their mortifications, the number of their good works, the fervor of their prayers. As for me, O my God, in my very confidence lies all my hope. "For you, O Lord, alone have established me in hope." This confidence can never be in vain. "No one who hopes in the Lord will ever be confounded."

I am assured, therefore, of my eternal happiness, for I firmly hope for it, and all my hope is in you. "In you,

O Lord, have I hoped; let me never be confounded" (Te Deum).

I know, alas! I know but too well that I am weak and frail; I know the power of temptation against the strongest virtue. I have seen stars fall from heaven and pillars of the firmament totter, but these do not alarm me. While I hope in you I am sheltered from all misfortune, and I am sure that my trust will endure, for I rely on you to sustain this unfailing hope. Finally, I know that my confidence cannot exceed your goodness and that I shall never receive less than I have hoped for from you. Therefore I hope that you will uphold me against my evil inclinations, protect me against the angry assaults of the evil one, and cause my weakness to triumph over my powerful enemies. I hope that you will never cease to love me, and that I shall love you unceasingly.

Saint Claude de la Colombiere, SJ

God's Dream for Me

Your dream, O Master, is to lay hold of me with your divine life.
Your dream is to purify me, to recreate me,
to make me a new person in your image.
Your dream is to fill me with your love, so that I love the Father
and all my brothers and sisters just as you do.
Your dream is to draw me to you with the closest of bonds,
to unite my heart with yours, to make me strong,
to impart to me your divine power
so that I can overcome evil and be constant in doing good.
Your dream is to inflame me with untiring zeal to spread your Kingdom.
Your dream is to possess me in this life and in the life to come.
May your dream come true! May I be able to give all you ask of me. Amen.

Based on the writings of Blessed James Alberione

Cor Dulce, Cor Amabile (Dear Heart, Loving Heart)

Dear heart, loving Heart,
Wounded with love for us,
Stricken with love for us,
Be forgiving toward me.
Heart of Jesus, sweeter than honey,
Purer than the pure sun,
Sanctuary of God's temple,
Sum of God's treasures.
You are the harbor of a shipwrecked world,
Secure peace for the faithful,
Refuge for guilty minds,
Shelter for devout hearts.

Traditional Catholic Latin hymn

Prayer of Abandonment

Father, I abandon myself into your hands, do with me what you will.
Whatever you may do, I thank you: I am ready for all, I accept all.
Let only your will be done in me and in all your creatures.
I wish no more than this, O Lord. Into your hands, I commend my soul;
I offer it to you with all the love of my heart;

For I love you, Lord, and so need to give myself:
To surrender myself into your hands without reserve
and with boundless confidence. For you are my
Father.

Saint Charles de Foucauld

Act of Abandonment

O supreme goodness of the sovereign Providence of my God! I abandon myself forever into your arms. Whether gently or forcefully, lead me wherever you will. I will not consider the way through which you will have me pass; rather, I will keep my eyes fixed on you, my God, who guide me. My soul finds no rest without the arms and the heart of this heavenly Providence, my true mother, my strength and my defense. Therefore, I resolve with your divine assistance, O my Savior, to follow your desires and your decrees, without regarding or examining why you do this rather than that: I will blindly follow you according to your divine will, without seeking my own inclinations.

Thus, I am determined to leave everything to you, taking no part therein but keeping myself peacefully in your arms, desiring nothing except what you inspire me to desire, to will, to wish. I offer you this desire, O my

God, beseeching you to bless it. I accept everything it includes, relying on your goodness, liberality, and mercy, with wholehearted confidence in you, distrust of myself, and knowledge of my great misery and frailty.

Saint Jane Frances de Chantal

Pauline
BOOKS & MEDIA

A mission of the Daughters of St. Paul

As apostles of Jesus Christ,
evangelizing today's world:

We are CALLED to holiness
by God's living Word and Eucharist.

We COMMUNICATE the Gospel message
through our lives and through all
available forms of media.

We SERVE the Church
by responding to the hopes and needs
of all people with the Word of God,
in the spirit of St. Paul.

For more information visit us at:
www.pauline.org